1

2024년
the year 2024

a small catalogue of thoughts
on forward motion
while traveling

by sabina petra

Book Cover by Sabina Petra / Photographs by Sabina Petra

1st edition 2025

ISBN 979-8-9926389-2-9

1. 봄 (spring)   ten poems

2. 여름 (summer)   thirteen poems

3. 가을 (autumn)   fourteen poems

4. 겨울 (winter)   thirteen poems

1. 봄 (spring)

suzhou
beijing
busan
hong kong

one.

it's just
truly
it's not fair
like why
is your hair so shiny
so deep black
ugh
so pretty
why
are you like bread?
you have a crust but
on the inside
it's all soft and doughy
you probably smell good too
i want to
smell
the hollow of your neck
the crook of your arm
the palm of your hand when you
wake up in the morning
curled around my shoulder
a thumb underneath my jaw

why
are you so cocky yet
so funny
running around like a child
playing ninja
i spread my arms in answer
playing a plane
we are silly together
why
is that so easy?

why are your eyes so open and
full of surprise when they see me?

truly
why
do you like her more?
she's not generous nor kind
and you haven't kissed me yet
i mean
that should really sway you
i'm a good kisser
did you see my lips all plump and soft
against your friend's cheek?
could you tear your eyes away from it?
you want that
right?

i wonder if you look at me and think;
it's just
truly
it's not fair
like why
are her eyes like the ocean?
her hair like the wind?
why is her skin like milk
why do her teeth look as if they can make the sound of laughter by
themselves?
why is her heart so big?
why can't i nestle in there
and make myself a home?

it's my home
that heart
mine
and

you're invited
but
you'll have to cross the threshold
if you hold back,
we'll just be pals
and truly
why
want more than that?
you're great as you are
and i am great as i am
hello there friend
how lovely to share a day with you
your hair is so shiny

two.

every time i eat good korean food
real korean food
i want to cry
because it feels like i've been cold for so long
i had forgotten i was frozen
until this food thaws me
from the inside
and glaciers come out

it's like a winter meal from my childhood
after a day of skating
it was fun but you're so cold it hurts
cheeks chafed and feet aching
your hands like little claws that can barely grip a spoon
your legs itching from sudden temperature change
now that you're near the hearth
your ears glowing

then you eat
and the ice inside cracks
it's painful and intensely satisfying

three.

i am leaving
i'm not quite sure how this country and its people
got to be
got to feel
so important to me
leaving other places was easier

have i changed while i was here?
apparently - so i've been told
and if i've evolved in some way
did the world around us level up as well?

i have traveled so many roads
shared so many dinners
perused so many malls for a random archery lane
i've ordered so many cheap taxis
had my picture taken by strangers
and my passport scanned more
in 6 months
than in my entire lifetime before that
i've said so many prayers
played so many shows
looked for so much korean food
to find the real deal only twice
got hair treatments and foot massages
sang karaoke and drank too much plum wine
looked at palaces and temples but most of all mountains
and more mountains
and lakes with mountains
taken so many flights
seen so many airports
with so much security

cameras and officers and soldiers and metal detectors and id checks
pat-downs and face recognitions
i've had so many small talks snuck into free seconds
so many small questions asked an answered
so many small cultural behaviors probed and unraveled
so many words translated
so many translator apps wrestled with
sentences and words slowed down
simplified
until only their very essence remained
stripped of all beauty or embellishment
of all nuance or refinement
until you can only communicate with yes and no
good and bad
and some crude body language
yet somehow you still make friends and lovers and family
so many times i wondered whether we actually
understood each other
whether you were angry or happy or tired
trying to read between the lines and take in
a complete and complex person at a glance

i've learned how to step away
before i gave you too much power
before i got swallowed up by my aim to please you
i've learned how to be content with loving
to be proud of it
of how it makes a couple of months full
instead of empty
i've learned i like to slow down
and that it's better to stoke a sun
than a wildfire
better some coals
than a pool of gasoline

i've learned i like happy drunks
content and kind and jolly
that anger and trauma lies under the surface of many
who never dared to face the pain of it

i've learned that a country is beautiful
no matter its flaws
even if you feel like you've seen
more beauty elsewhere
that the scenery or the food or the company
a custom a scent a fabric a sound
can get drawn on you like wood grain
can take hold of you like roots
making you understand you're all closer
and more colorful and different
than you've ever imagined
and that understanding
is the loudest language

but now
i have to take responsibility for my life

if i had stayed
we would've continued to have fun
talks
hot pot
late night massages
laughter and drinks and archery
but while some things are beautiful in the making
in order to finish it
to truly make it edible
you need to bake it
put it in the oven and let it transform
like cake

if i had stayed
i would've learned the same lesson over and over
swam in sweet batter forever
the absence of a change or growth
the absence of a new challenge, a new love, a new heart
would've made me severely unhappy
i have to walk away with a cake
with a full belly

i am leaving
bye china
bye mountains
bye lakes
bye mystical past and polluted present
bye lights and watertowns
tourist traps and dumpling houses
bye hotpot under the stars
bye bustling trains and cigarette smoke and day-long adventures
bye random noodle shacks and staring children with
round pink peach cheeks
bye people touching my hair and asking me if i'm blind
bye mist and clouds and pagodas and pandas

bye my friends, my family
i will miss you
this is the right, the correct, the only natural following sentiment
for all of us

four.

round and round the cup i go
my finger on the rim and
my upper lip in the liquid

round and round my mind i go
my hand grasping yours and
my lips kissing air

five.

my mind is the eye of a storm
it's quiet in there
i don't want to reach out and feel the whirlwind on the edges
get ripped away into the stream

it whispers around me
that wind
it whispers of other people
how i need them
how i've turned from them
how i'm hiding

i am
i am hiding
i am hiding from being overlooked
i am hiding
from being left

i'm hiding
from telling you how lucky you are
how lonely i am
from making this a big deal
which it is
i know it is
i simply don't want it to be
i can't face it just yet

i am hiding
in the quiet
until the storm closes in

21

six.

i breathed
and i cried
i sat on my knees
i'm still not used to it
but they didn't hurt this time
in the centuries old building
in the centuries old mountains
with a centuries old faith
uttering a centuries old wish

please teach me mercy towards myself
mercy towards others
please
let me finally take part in life
and not be afraid to never start
let me trust
and accept
something i've always claimed but have never done

the centuries old wish
for love
love
love

seven.

you don't sit next to me on the bus
you talk with an energy that seems almost designed
for me to hear it
to a point where it becomes annoyingly penetrating
you don't invite me to dinners
don't step into an elevator with me
you pointedly walk past me in a hurry
almost at every turn you
seem to disappear from my sight

but
do i disappear from your thought?

you sometimes look at me
with a gaze so intent
and direct
it kind of startles me
a smirk halfway up your lips
a hello halfway down your tongue
you dawdle
talk a little louder
sit a little straighter
you simply don't succeed in looking away
you put a hand on my shoulder or let me step in the car first or
tell me i'm beautiful when you're drunk in a very
          matter of fact these are the ways of the world and don't you
          forget it
kind of way

sure
maybe you were startled by the sea-colored eyes
it made you realize
how different from you i look

but i'd like to think i know something
that i am right about one damn thing in my life
that in all the times i never knew if someone was watching
in all the times i was hoping for affection
or loving without response
i learned when it was actually happening
i'd like to think that in these mere seconds i understand
that you like me
you like me
you don't want to
but you do
you damn cute boy
damn cute chinese man with your korean haircut and your left ear full of
silver earrings
your lisp and your pine needle eyes and your cocky strut
you damn cute boy you like me
and you think i'm damn cute too

guess what
cocky motherfucker
i am

eight.

i'm standing on the side of a road
such a colorful road
red neon signs and yellow billboards
green traffic signs and behind me
the sounds of a
saxophone
playing "'isn't she lovely"
i'm sipping a sugar bubble tea
it's warm and cold and sweet all at once
sweat runs down my back
sticking the sheer cotton shirt to my skin

i'm taking my time looking around
there are locals here and i am not one of them
there are tourists here and i am not one of them
it's strange having traveled so far and for so long
that there is a part in every country that seems familiar
and a part in every country that seems new

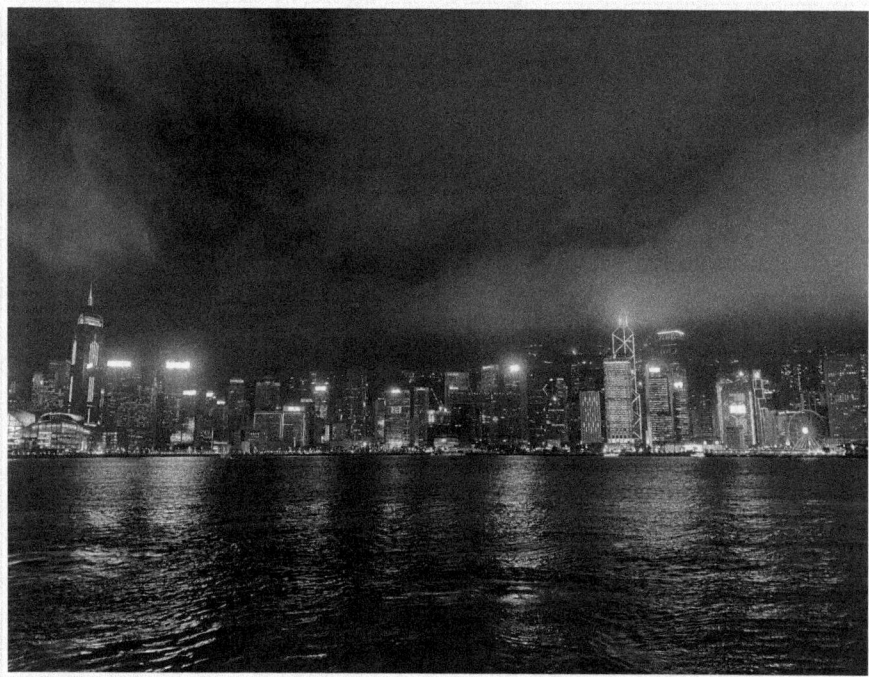

nine.

i have taken a day off
it is very unusual for me to do so
for anyone in the theatre industry to do so
but it was time
and i took a day off

all my colleagues are at work
and i am sitting on the hotel roof deck
looking at the city across the harbor

there's a family dining on the floor below me
outside near the grills
all ages
elders chatting and drinking
parents prepping and cutting
children chasing each other
squealing and laughing
pausing only for a snack
until the real meal is ready

i remember being part of a family like that
my opa in his big leather chair
drinking the tiniest glass of jenever
handing me an advocaatje with whipped cream
offering my mother a larger amount to appease her
as if she would ever not let me have it
i would be running around the table
occasionally grabbing a handful of crisps or nuts
while aunts and uncles cut cheese and vegetables in the kitchen
stirring the chicken soup
and oma is holding court in the middle of the living room
hoarding stories she can tell her neighbors with pride the next day
guarding the fancy cookie jar

right now
that whole family has fallen apart
both oma and opa are gone and are no longer holding court
or, with gleeful smiles and shining apple cheeks,
giving out liquor to children
the aunts and uncles are angry at each other and
the children i used to run around the table with
are strangers to me now
i don't know what lives they live
what fills their days
or dreams
if they have children of their own
i don't think that if we saw each other
we would be able to smile at one another from across the grill
rejoicing in a shared meal
it would be a cold room
with icy stares
and chilly silences

i am sad i am not part of a family
even as a child i remember
when it was all slipping away from me
how sad i was to see it go
all i wanted was for us to be together
and celebrate
celebrating was so important to me
but i am happy i am free of them
i can be in a warm continent and enjoy spicy food and
sweat through my afternoons
instead of sitting in the icebox that is my home

the juxtaposition of my life is not lost on me
in fact
it stares me in the face every day

ten.

jungkook
정국 씨
has been recorded and watched almost his entire life
people seem surprised and often
downright elated
to find that he
has a temper
can't take a loss
can be sensual
let's say: extremely horny
is silly
is quiet
acts like a little boy
dances to his own music in his room
can take criticism
is sweet
kind
a bully
cares deeply for his brothers
looks out for others
is lazy
works hard
can't get out of bed
dances harder
lets the world slide off his shoulders
cries often
is vain
doesn't care
is confident
is uncomfortable
speaks the truth
hides
in other words

is a human being
of course he is
no one is one thing
not even jungkook

i feel like i don't have that privilege
maybe because i've created expectations
or
expectations have been created for me
but
i can't be any of those things
except nice
and happy
if i have a temper
i'm a bitch
if i am horny
i'm a slut
if i'm silly
i'm a child
if i'm quiet
i'm stupid
if i'm lazy
i deserve to be alone
if i work hard
i deserve to be alone
if i let the world slide off
i'm cold
if i cry often
i'm crazy
if i'm vain
i'm not real
if i don't care
i'm not desirable
if i speak the truth
i'm rude

if i hide
i'm a coward

but i can be nice
and happy
and they like that version
but in all honesty
who really does?
that sounds fucking boring
and kinda scary
all the other versions sounds more
appealing to me

jungkook ssi
you have, in a way,
reminded me
that being all these things is a blessing
a very powerful and positive thing
and i should be celebrated for it

2. 여름 (summer)

hong kong
seoul

one.

i walk through a deserted street
on top of a hill in the middle of seoul city
the buildings are condemned
low stone structures with grey and blue-tiled roofs
crisscrossed with yellow tape yelling "danger!" at me
the innards of the houses lay in the street for vultures to pick on
discarded dining trays, closets, couches
clothes, mops, shelves
the odd toilet bowl
the city is roaring around this hill but here
life has disappeared
but for a pigeon or two
and the unseen scurry of a rat

suddenly
through the music on my headphones
i hear a knocking
a pounding

i turn off the music and try to locate the sound
behind a door
someone is in one of these buildings
muttering a string of incomprehensible words

i don't know if the person has seen me through the key-hole
and is trying to get my attention
or if this person is talking to someone else
or on the phone
if it's a handy man doing his part for the demolition
or a homeless person
mad with hunger and addiction
or loneliness and loss
the korean words are foreign to me

and i am scared
in this abandoned lot full of debris
i find myself inching away from the door

but
but but
it is a human voice
and what if they need help?

suddenly i recognize the word
i think it is a woman
i think she is older
but the word is something a child would utter

아버지 아버지 아버지

aboji aboji aboji
father father father

over and over and over again
as she pounds on the door
i don't know if the little girl in her
is yelling for her dad or
if the older woman in her
is pleading with her God but
i know i have to try and help
even if someone lunges at me the moment i open the door

so i go over
and try the door
it seems locked
but as i pull it
there is a slight give
so i tug at it with all i've got and
and it opens

behind it i find
a woman in her 80s
sitting on her walker
blinking in the fierce sunlight as it streams into the minuscule hallway
she is confused by this blonde woman staring down at her
as confused as i am to find her
and we look non plussed at each other for a bit
then she thanks me
and says different things i don't understand
i forget to ask her how she is
if she needs anything
if i can call anyone
i just bow and say
      don't worry about it
      아니에요
and i wish her a happy weekend
and then go on my way

as i turn i find a tear streaking my cheek
i think to myself
the world isn't scary at all
the world just needs help

two.

you run towards me
down the sloping path
your feet slapping heavily on the pavement

i stay to the shoulder of the road
near the bright lilac flowers
while two ajummas are chatting on the other side
plenty of room for you to hurtle yourself through

but your path arcs a bit
i see you glance up and maybe the sun is in your eyes but
i have a feeling you can see me
and you veer so heavily in my direction that
for a moment
i think your going to run straight into me

you pass me with perhaps 3 cm to spare
your square, sturdy body
leaves a wind in its wake
as solid as the real thing
it slams me in the chest
with the equal amount of muscle
as if you had embraced me

i cannot say at all that it was displeasing

three.

you age in layers

you don't just grow older
you layer year on top of year
like an onion
like spekkoek
i am not simply 43 years old
i have 43 layers
and i can see and feel the 27th
as well as the 34th
and the 40th

and i will keep stacking

four.

you smile gently at me
with those goose down lips
and those velvet eyes

i wonder what's coming
i mean
you are a bank teller
who just told me
that there is nothing you can do for me
no residency means
no account

but somehow you're worried
i'm staying in seoul for a while
and you don't trust how much i have to pay my landlord
i could explain to you that it's okay
i trust my landlord
but there is simply not enough time or
acquaintance for that
so i just smile back at you
waiting

then
looking sideways
and back at me
you lean forward and softly say
        is there not somewhere else you can stay?
        can you find a hotel?

so concerned
i don't think you know how old i am
how far i've traveled
and how many places i have stayed in
i think you think i'm new to this

and you feel protective
you can't be more than 31
it's cute

i try to smile as softly as you have spoken
and tell you
that i will look into it

i thank you for your help
and your excellent english
i bow
and i leave

i feel better
i got nothing done at the bank
but someone tried to look out for me
and it felt really good

five.

men everywhere
men in starched oversized black t shirts
with the ends of their short sleeves neatly folded
men in ironed jeans and sneakers
men with postures straight as candles
with haircuts sharp as razors
their hair shiny like soft silk
and hands smooth and manicured
men with inscrutable stares and full lips
with strong broad backs and long arms
perfect for embracing
men with rumbling voices
you feel vibrating in your sternum
with long paces and a solidity about them
that puts them squarely into this world

men moving in packs
wearing their camaraderie as armor
laughing and talking loudly
finding the freedom to look and disapprove
men sitting alone on stoops
wearing their solitude as armor
haughty in their stillness
shrugging off the world as if it doesn't matter

men with egos
men with soft hearts
men who can show them
men who cannot
men with pride
men with self respect
men with boundaries
men with simmering ideas

they are all so intimidating
i calm myself with the thought that when
i finally slip my hand in yours
there is absolutely nothing to be scared of
and i can find immense joy in knowing
that for all the armored exteriors
we tend to be molten inside

i will run my hand through your hair like silk
bury my face in your starched black shirt
let my bones reverberate along with your
low rumble

at the moment
i am simply holding hands with
myself
and that's okay
i'm cheerful company

six.

i am angry, i suppose
at how long it is taking the universe to fulfill
that one simple wish i've had since childhood
to not be alone
i am angry and in my anger
i see things around me that confirm it
people start looking at me with hostile glances
they get in the way and move too slowly and behave rudely

it is funny because i also
as of today
am pretty sure i have another job lined up
a home to come back to
i sang today and talked to my mother and did my laundry
and nothing about this day was all that bad

i think this anger is so deep and old
that whenever it bubbles through the cracks it has
the pressure of time behind it
like volcanoes
it's not that we don't like fire
hearths and campfires and pizza ovens
it's just that we don't like them engulfing us
anger can be useful
purpose and will power and defense mechanism
it's the engulfing of the day
of my heart
that does me in

seven.

the heavens are crying
weeping

i might as well
join them

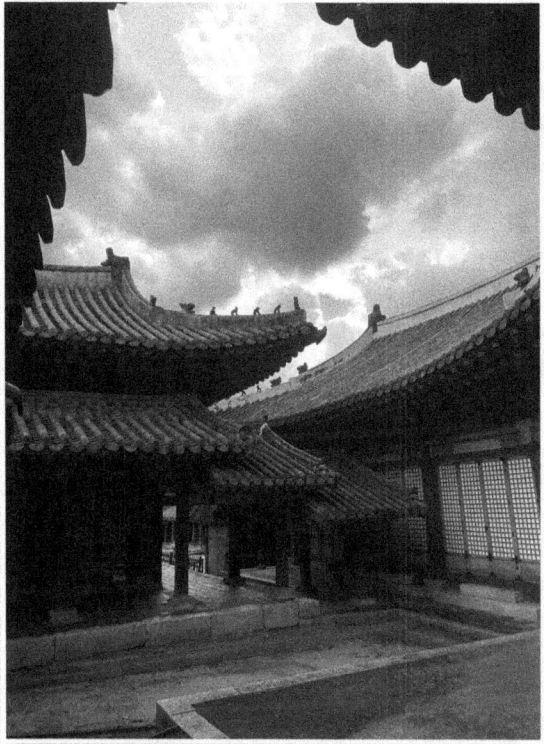

eight.

some things i've learned in my first week in korea

when you stand tall
the sun shines brighter
more people open their heart to you
they believe your good intentions

when you speak louder
people will slow down to listen to you

when you dance in the street
and you don't judge yourself
it will be met with joy
it'll drastically change your mood
your day
your life

being with someone is wonderful
and true love is the ultimate goal
but being with someone who doesn't fit
is way worse than being alone
and the freedom and possibility that comes with my own
place and space and pace
is quite lovely
it only becomes more inviting
to the person who belongs with me here

things will come to me
love will come to me
i don't have to try or search
but for someone who is not trying or searching
i sure am sizing up a loooooot of beautiful men
so many are
very beautiful

i sweat
a lot
there's not a lot i can do about it
so i might as well keep standing up tall

soil matters
in hong kong i was considerably content
but my feet and the soil spoke different languages
even if our tongues did not

here
the language is the biggest hurdle
but my feet understand the earth
and this earth recognizes my feet
home
home home home
i had almost forgotten
how beautiful that feels

nine.

people who make a big deal
out of elbowing their way to the door of the train
as it pulls into the station
have a responsibility to
keep a damn pace once they get out of it

ten.

there's a boy
a man
with a boy's energy
a boy
on the train
he's taller than most
wide shoulders in a white t-shirt
square jaw
and full lips

he smiles at me
wait
is he smiling at me?
no idea
the train is very full and i am
quite far away from him
swaying to the music in my headphones
i tend to do that
dance on the train
and it looks like
he's doing the same thing
listening to music and bobbing his head
maybe he's just smiling to his tune
or at his friend talking to him
he's so tall that the smile works like a lighthouse
casting further than intended
it's probably not for me
but for a different ship altogether
and so in a split second i decide
i don't reciprocate
and look away

two stations later we have moved closer together
still a good pack of about 10 people between us
i look over and this time
there is no mistaking it
i move my shoulders to the music
he sees it
and he smiles
a brilliant, wide, toothy smile

this is strange
smiling at strangers is not very common here
and dancing on the train is something
i've never seen anyone else do
but i recognize this kindred spirit
a wild card in his culture
and so i smile back
just as wide and toothy

suddenly a connection is made
over the heads of a dozen unaware people
as we bop to our own beats
in our private disco

when he leaves the train
he takes out an earphone
turns around and grins at me
waves

i made a friend
a friend who feels like an old one already
i will probably never see him again
but i hope i do

eleven.

it is strange how something as small as
altered plans and an unanswered message
sends me in a complete tailspin
the fear of being abandoned
left behind - forgotten - never needed
is so real
the nerve so much more exposed than i had imagined
it's easy to be strong, you see
in a daily life
when you have no one to disappoint you
but when you're dealing with other human beings
suddenly the possibility
of being put by the wayside
is here

of course so is the possibility of love and connection
but fear doesn't think of that
there is no need for protection from connection
fear is there to protect
and she has her hackles raised
her fists up
her boxing stance ready

i plant my bare feet on the damp tiny yellow tiles of the bathroom
i realize
it would be nice to act again
to tell a story with others
to connect again
i have been doing life on my own for quite a while now
maybe it's time to let others in and
create a tapestry together
instead of this tightly knotted piece of yarn i've made
by myself

a private moment
my teacher called it
a stanislavsky thing
where you are private in public
i used to love that stuff
unapologetically showing your heart
without being judged for it
having been raised in a household where being heard by the neighbors
was the biggest sin
it was such a relief

i wiggle my toes against the ceramic
and what starts as a couple of tears
suddenly becomes a flood
i open my mouth
i take a leaf out of the book of korean culture
and i wail
i wail as much as my dutch voice will let me
i wail to try and get the grief and loneliness out
i wail to release the fear and sadness that has been gripping me
if i can turn it all into sound and let it leave my body
i can finally take a new breath
but it is restricted, still
it can't reach as far and as high as i want it to
it's floating out of the tiny bathroom window
into the dark seoul alley behind my apartment

i wonder if it actually reaches anyone's ears
no one is listening
still
still no one is listening
perhaps if i can be louder
i can reach the heavens
or my ancestors
i stretch my neck and clench my eyes

my face glazed with salt
howling up at the stars
my grandmother probably thinking
    oh shut up already
    it's not like you're living through a war
no i am not
but loneliness is an inner war of sorts
one that no one knows you're fighting

i think of my great-grandmother
who told my father she thought he was too harsh on me
that sweet woman
she did live through a war and yet she knew what modern harshness was
she used to fold her lips inward a bit as she kissed you hello
and then proceed to give you 10 kisses in quick succession
with this rapidly popping sound
her signature greeting
i wish i could tell my children about her
and about my other great-grandmother who was an amazing cook
who had a large chest that she called her "candy table"
because it could hold a saucer of licorice
about my great-grandfather who was a baker
and sold his freshly baked bread off a bike with a huge basket in front
how he would give my father a bun
he would open it and put a pad of butter in the still steaming center
then pour caster sugar on it
it would be the best thing my father had ever tasted in his life
about my grandmother the painter and my grandmother the cuddler
who had a sheet of loose soft skin dangling from her upper arms
while she was darning socks my mother used to play with it
i am so sad that i won't be able to
continue these stories for them
as i realize i will not be the only one forgotten here

my wails have quieted
i am not nearly done but
i am tired
it's like i have been screaming for a while
if no one answers the point gets lost

i wonder if someone passed my apartment tonight
and felt a little ache in their hearts
an echo of what i was feeling

because as alone as i am
grief is for certain
a universal thing

55

twelve.

think about it this way;
if you don't find someone suitable to stare at on your train ride
you get to focus all of that reserved love
on yourself

nice

thirteen.

the grey stones on this street are broken up by
a bright red sewer lid
as a kid i always avoided stepping on those
i actually still do
because i didn't want to
"fall into a well"
metaphorically
and i thought i'd be inviting it if i'd step on it
so i would hop over

today
i stepped right in the middle of the lid
with determination
because whatever happens
i choose red over grey

3. 가을 (autumn)

**lynchburg, va
seoul**

one.

as i walk down the stairs
into the depths of the subway
i get swallowed up in a sea of black and grey and tan
and i wonder if someone sees this one lone
bright pink boat
in green shoes

two.

i was angry to be there
fucking bustling overpriced house of snobs
where i can't even exchange a pair of pants because
it's been over a week
a week!
and the tag's not attached
i have it
the tag
but it's not attached
nothing they can do
so sorry
bullshit
well
i guess i'll do some groceries and
get the fuck out of here

in a romcom
i would bump into someone who was dragged there by his friends
equally bummed to be at the palace of snootiness
and we would angrily grab the same piece of clothing or
violently bust into each other and
the whole day would turn around
shared misery makes good romcom i guess

but instead
i'm just a bitter woman waiting for the bus in 100 degree shade
it would've been better to take a breath
recognize where i am and what i want
instead of wildly staring around me for a clue to life
the world isn't going asunder
i'll just find a tailor
that's it
they're still a good pair of pants

regroup
reroute
then perhaps if i do meet someone
who's also calmly reassessing
we could be happy together
instead of unhappy together
i've done the unhappy part already
no need for a rerun

when i am calm like that
when i find that pocket of truth
that eye in the storm
i can simply look at people for their beauty
instead of their compatibility
and whether or not i'm striking the right vibe
pose
tune
whether or not i have enough lipstick on or
my sweaty pits aren't too visible
everyone is so beautiful
you have the classic young shape of faces and swoosh of lashes and
sweeps of hair but
there are so many quirky funny joyful kind wise interesting faces where i
want to ask them immediately
what their whole life story is

and
there is a beautiful man on the bus
tall and strong and young with a
round face like a bao
kind chocolatey eyes
he just got a haircut and is completely clad in
very dark denim
and his arms
they look so soft

the kind that has a lot of muscle underneath
but is layered on top with a blanket of good food and mother's love or
something
they are so beautiful
he catches me looking
and i don't look away
or smile
i just look
i briefly wonder if i'm being creepy
but i also don't care
people are beautiful
i want to drink it in
without trying to be perceived a certain way
i know myself
that's enough

we get off at the same stop
he books it out of the bus and across the road
it's hot as balls outside and he is in full denim
button-down buttoned all the way up
those big loose pants that are the style here
how he manages to run in this heat
is beyond me

i'm sure as fuck not running
but then i see we have to catch the same bus
well he's gonna make it
i'm not
good for him
the line for this bus is long
it takes a while for people to get in
and wouldn't you know it
i'm the last yokel who squeezes herself in between a poor young man and
the door
right next to the disgruntled driver

i almost topple back out
i make a face
        oops this is scary
and soft-arms-guy
-himself sandwiched between a gaggle of sweaty students and an old lady
dressed in flower patterns and a huge wicker hat who snatched the last seat-
turns around at that moment and catches it
and smiles
i smile back
ever so briefly
before the unfortunate man i'm sweating up against starts a conversation
about san francisco of all places
and soft-arms-guy is out of reach and out of the bus and out of my life
before we ever had the chance to
i don't know
exchange fore arm freckle patterns
or something

the guy i'm talking to seems nervous
the lenses of his glasses are scratched
and his teeth are crooked
he is incredibly kind and curious
and awkward and a little funny
probably very sweet
and i'm grateful for his conversation because
the more he frets the calmer i get in comparison
to make up for
to keep the balance
or something
and i find my own rhythm
my own tone of voice

i realize the more i
recognize myself
the more others

recognize me
gotta be known to make yourself known
kinda thing

67

three.

if i have to hear
        you are so wonderful
        you are so great
        you are magnificent and magical
        and probably the best person to love me ever
        BUT
on more fucking time

i'm gonna pull some hair out
and it won't be mine

four.

i'm quite tricky
aren't i
endless seas of kindness but
a temper as high as the himalayas
and as hot as death valley

patience for anyone but myself however
come at me and i will defend myself to the death
because i know the core to be intricate
made of molten gold
sun-like
planet-core

so many dreams and so little time and
a great desire to sit on my butt for at least 3 hours a day
everything is all or nothing
stop or go
dancing in the street or
crying on the bus

i don't judge people by their appearance but
every word uttered triggers an opinion

i'm incredibly positive and incredibly sad
i am very brave and scared all the time
i at once believe i can do anything with the universe at my back
and that i am all alone and will one day disappear like a wisp of wind

but i do like myself
and i am proud of who i've become
as juxtaposed as i am
like my life

and there is someone who needs me
as much as i need them
i may want to reach out to hold their hand yet
they are reaching just as hard to find mine
and together we can be
tricky
and
happy

five.

when i think back on it

i think my grandmother was probably one of the smartest
and strongest people i knew

it was never very evident because
it was hidden behind her husband and her children
her vanity and her fear of crowds

but when her husband died and her children left
and the crowd coming to visit her was the only thing really sustaining her
she showed her strength

her strength was listening
taking in all the information
and storing it
filing it
comparing it and weighing it
never forgetting a thing

even in the last hours of her life she
asked me questions about the universe
scraping the last facts
squeezing the last bit of connection
from this world
before taking a conscious leap
without fear

she was a vessel of knowledge
and not really afraid of anything
even thought we all thought she was
she was quietly amassing
a life worth living
until she had enough

72

six.

wat is er kind	what is it child
ik ben zo verdrietig oma wat moet ik doen?	i am so sad grandma what should i do?
waarom ben je verdrietig dan schat	why are you sad then treasure
ik ben heel erg eenzaam	i am very lonely
heb je niemand?	don't you have anyone?
nee	no
kun je niet met je moeder praten?	can't you talk with your mother?
nee	no
denk dat er niemand gaat komen?	do you think no one will come?
ik hoop ik hoop maar ik ben zo bang dat er niemand gaat komen bent u gelukkig oma en kunt u iemand naar mij sturen?	i hope i hope but i am so afraid that no one will come are you happy grandma and can you send me someone?
ik ben gelukkig kind wil je een kop melk?	i am happy child do you want a cup of milk?
nee dank u	no thank you

74

so many translation hurdles to take
                    do you have a boyfriend?
        no
my mouth said that word but i think my face said;
        i'm heartbroken
he replied
                    so not yet
        yeah not yet
i was wondering whether it was appropriate for me to say
that i had been married but then i thought:
let's start over fresh shall we
why should that be such a sturdy part of my existence
let it be like ice cream
melting away as my life gets hotter

                    do you want a korean guy?
jeez i never knew people here could be so direct
okay
let's roll with it
        yeah sure
        i want to stay here
        i could practice my korean

                        maybe you can meet someone at the gym
i laughed
one single cackle
i mean come on
are you trying to embarrass me?
all the guys from the gym are here!
why out me on the spot like that
that's basically announcing to the room:
here i am take me
but then again

all the boys in this room are paired up
so maybe
he means when a fresh batch comes in
        haha yeah maybe

i don't think i felt that drunk at all
but i don't remember how the topic changed after that
about 20 someks and 4 hours of sleep later
everything i've said is a blur
swimming around my head like the seafood we had
before it was food
i'm so hungover
my skin really didn't like my adventure
stretching over my face like salt water taffy
but my soul did

it was an ultimate exercise
in friendship
understanding that it's the lifeblood of this culture
without friends you have no
food
laughter
jobs
recommendations
life
and ultimately
love comes from friendship too

i cannot think that just because love won't find me
i'm not worth finding
all these friends have found me
it's a different kind of treasure
all this searching for something more elite made me forget
how important this is
caviar is great but i really like a good stew

and in the end
that's what you live on
stew
not little fish eggs

i mean the fact that i'm swaying to music on the train
on a queasy empty stomach and a sore voice
and 4 hours of sleep
with a smile on my face
remembering how i sang "somebody to love" with a couple of new friends
who were all older than me yet too shy to talk to me
i still don't know any of their names -
a good heart and a glass of beer is the same as understanding a sentence
it means i have family now
i'm backed up
i have a clan
a tribe
and how can i leave now?
i want to never

eight.

i judge my timeline
by airplane lavatory mirrors
every time i catch myself in one of those
it's a reminder of how time has gone past

on a short hop from one asian city to another
i never had to check
it's the big intercontinental flights
the one crossing oceans and longitudes
where i cross my own borders as well
and see more timelines appear on my face

telling me that yes
i've grown older
yes
time is passing
yes
you're wiser
yes
it's running out

nine.

we always think we are the only ones hurting
when someone leaves we are the only ones left behind

i wonder though
what happens on the other side
whether someone breaks their own heart

out of guilt
knowing it was a mistake
or a necessary loss
out of the missing of the person
the you-shaped hole in their horizon
that can never really be filled
and will stay a shadow until the last of their days

when they look at the sun there is always
a part of it that doesn't shine

we never hear about that

ten.

there was something so beautiful and familiar
about his tears

they weren't self-pitying
and they weren't necessarily
pouring out of his face

they were pouring out of his heart
it was a simple confession and its result;
that he tried so hard not to
but couldn't manage
to love her more than he wanted to
to need her more than he wanted to

and the simple grief of a possibility slipping from his fingers

beyond all war and death and despair
and poverty and loneliness and pain
there is a special patch of salt
especially reserved for the tears of unrequited love

81

eleven.

it strange how we only see elderly people by that identity;
old
we cannot see that they've embodied everything in this life;
from a squirmy baby to an energetic kid to a sexual twenty-something
a mother a friend a sister a worker with a dream and a purpose

all we see is ineptitude
pain and wrinkles
the stiffness of their movements and their furrowed brow
i hope that when someone looks into my eyes at that age
they see
me then
and all the decades before

twelve.

koreans often talk of their first love
and how important it is

when i look back i had many obsessions
i remember the first boy i was infatuated with
i was four
was that my first love?
i don't think i knew what love was
or was that its' purest form?

i remember the boy in 12th grade
in the netherlands you are about 11 at that time
his face full of joyful freckles and his mop of brown hair
i don't think he has any of that hair now
it was incredibly one-sided
is that love?

the first time i slowly fell in love with someone
i was 13 then
and we actually did date for a whopping 2 months
my heart was full of him
he would sometimes talk of marriage and somehow
that seemed wildly ridiculous to me

when we broke up i couldn't let him go
my hands released but my mind clung on
i ended up setting him up with what would later become his wife
knowing it would never be me
and that at least this way i had some hand in it
is that love?
the giving away kind?
the giving up kind?
the meddling kind?

my first kiss and first sex with the boy i adored
but grew restless with because i felt i was
constantly taking care of him
he was probably the kindest boy i had ever met
but i was wild and he was calm
and i wanted to overstep our boundaries

the relationship where i just wanted attention and then
the relationship where i decided to love someone
        decided to love
that sounds wrong, right?
i kept that up for the longest of all
because once i decide something
i mostly stick with it

and then the relationship that was all sorts of wrong but
so sexually charged

could it be
that at this age
i have still not truly felt
what love feels like?
what being loved feels like?
it is incredibly sad and frustrating and also
is that an exciting thing?
is everything still to come?

jeez let it come already
you slow motherfucker

84

thirteen.

as i press my forehead against the glass in order to
look outside of the dark window
i see a man there on a bicycle
in the middle of a traffic-filled road
the red and yellow lights flash around him
he is clad in a skintight green cycling uniform
he is tall and muscular
he's got this

he weaves around our bus and books it up the hill
to the roundabout
where even more traffic mills around
absolutely unfazed

i follow his path for as long as i can
until he is out of sight
i am amazed at his strength
and his bravery

he will never know i saw him
and marveled at him

i wonder how many people see me
dancing in the street like a 바보
and it fills their day in a way
i never expected

fourteen.

when i see other lives
play out in the preconceived pattern
a fist reaches in and squeezes my lungs tightly
am i missing something?
am i doing something wrong?

but what happens, happens
and nothing i could've done would have made my life
a usual one

4. 겨울 (winter)

shenzen
hangzhou
huangshan
wuzhen
guangzhou
ningbo
nanchang
shanghai
suzhou
seoul

one.

china is so beautiful
i can see how it was a land of mystery and dreams
dragons with steaming nostrils and
lakes with hidden magic properties
portals and tea houses and majestic bridges
now
you have to pay for every step into history or nature
the smog has replaced the steaming nostrils
the oily food will rob you of your magic properties
it's like the mystery disappeared
the moment it stopped sharing it

two.

i want to
grab that mop of jet black hair
it looks thick
i wonder how deeply my hand would sink into it
i want to grab a fistful of it
and yank it
not so hard that your neck will snap backward
i can issue control
i will not go too far
but a good short pull
i will softly bite your ear
then turn you around and
plant the most sensual kiss you ever had in your life
on your lips
firm but soft and a little tongue and a nip of the teeth

i will draw back to look in your eyes
smile with mine
before i kiss you again and this time
i'll anchor my hips to yours
then i'll pull away and squeeze that fist of hair for good measure
bite my lip and slap you hard on the chest

remember when we arm wrestled?
i'm strong
you're stronger
but no one ever gave this to you
i think you need it
little swagger boy
groin first
thinking you're hot than cold than hot again
wanting to get into my favor not caring
being sweet being aloof being kind being mean being shy being arrogant

inconsistent weirdo
don't think you've got me wound around your fingertips
i'm incredibly (dis)interested
i couldn't care more or less
you fascinate me
i'm just gonna smile at you
with my eyes

and in my mind
i'm yanking your hair

three.

does no one love me?

yes
answers the universe
i will give you signs that no one loves you

no one loves me

yes
answers the universe
i will make sure no one loves you

i want everyone to love me

yes
answers the universe
i will give you ways to ensure people love you

everybody loves me

yes
answers the universe
everyone loves you and you don't even have to try

so
in the meantime
when i am scared
and alone
am i not allowed to wonder
and cry
in case the universe hears me
and confirms it?

four.

who is that beautiful girl in the mirror
shaking her neon-pink panty-clad bootie?
she's dancing for nothing but the joy of it
for the rhythm of it
for the freeing feeling of being the best thing on earth
for the movement of it

how dare i ever think
i am not worth the most joyful attention
that i have to work for your approval
i have been approved
the universe has put a stamp right on my butt
look at what i can do
look at who i am
undeniably good

five.

i feel frozen inside
it won't melt
my body submerged in a hot bath
trying to release the shiver
building up within me

what is this?
this fear of what's to come?
what comes will come
it's as easy as that
but plans are addictive and goals give power
people around me seem hewn of stone
and i am wood
grown and warped by the elements
or air
a giant cumulus cloud threatening to rain
only to fly out to sea
on to some other land

the next step is closer than i think
i keep thinking i have to leap
but i really only need to step
or stumble

write
edit
learn
go
eat
practice
keep your mind and heart and eyes
open

you are here
not over there yet
if there's a reason to be here
then learn the lesson
why else
would you spend the time

melt, melt
don't be so afraid to
flow

six.

you said:
    like a lion
    roar
    brave;
    a challenge
    you face it

you looked at me with wonder
wide eyed
    what am i looking at?

force of nature baby
queen of the jungle
that's what

seven.

oh seriously
i want to scream at you right now

i understand that
from your point of view
you've had trials and tribulations
but didn't you make it?
didn't you find someone who
completely accepts you for who you are?
who you can trust,
be safe with,
be certain of?

i've never had that!
never!
ever!
i am ready to rip off every smile i see on every boy on the street
their self indulgent free spirited not a care in the world
full of glee with their easily gotten top prizes
i want to take a straw and slurp up their happiness to harness for my own
i am angry
so angry
i could jump up and tear the night sky from the heavens
in great big paper tatters

how dare you
how dare it be such an easy thing to find love
and how dare it be so elusive for me
how dare you say you've had it difficult
i've had nothing

i turn my head from the happy couples and
sniff my confidence back in through my nose
it rushes in cold like the weather

fine
i will just depend on myself
you can't depend on life to give you anything anyway

and then
i see a man walking past
early 30s, tall and handsome and well groomed
obviously in a good state of life
and yet an unmistakable air of anxiety wafts from him
a broken heart and a fluttering mind
i look at him
he glances my way and even his eye-roll tells me
that he really doesn't have the bandwidth to deal with the weird foreigner
right now
that i might be the last in a day full of hurdles
and yet i look at him steadfastly, even if he is not looking back
i want to telegraph to him that it's okay
that he'll be fine
that someone loves him
i am sure of it
even if it is me for a split second
i wonder if he can feel it

it weirdly restores my faith in the power of my own love
and at the same time
it angers me
i don't want to be on the look-out for the needy
i want to be one of those smiley motherfuckers
who thinks life is easy and wonderful

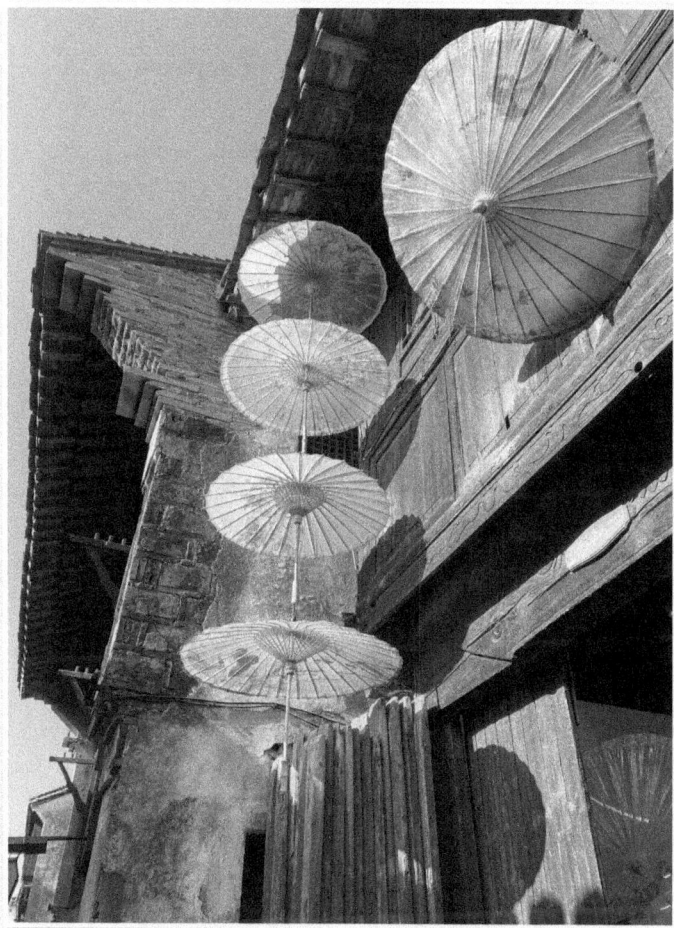

eight.

and all of a sudden the prayers have changed

yes i want
success and love and
health and the strength to trust myself and the universe
but

emergency has arisen
the world has become tangible all of a sudden
sounds of helicopters and
shouts in a language i barely understand
the news updating every minute and
opinions flying around my ears
instead of dreaming into the void of the open sky i
look to the buildings and see all the lives lived there
including mine
pinpricks of hope have become needles of fear

suddenly we are all connected by one thought:
what if our world goes asunder?
what if everything we thought of as normal and
a given
is pulled from us like a bad tablecloth trick?
i look at everyone grabbing their glass and plate
trying to save what they can
and my prayer is

please let us be safe
please
let us all be safe

nine.

i don't think a single day has passed
when i haven't thought of you

i met you once
for a total of perhaps
10 minutes
we were in the same subway car

for a total of perhaps
10 seconds
we had actual eye contact

and for a total of
6 months
you have stayed on my mind

i have never seen anyone like you
so openly joyful and kind
so happy to see someone else be
happy

i don't think a single day has passed
when i haven't wanted you to find me again

find me
make my heart burst open

ten.

i would live another day
just to hear music

eleven.

it is strange having to navigate
an unanswered prayer every day

or perhaps it is answered
without my knowledge

perhaps we crossed paths today
perhaps we do every day
and we simply do not notice

perhaps the universe is sighing and
rolling her eyes
at our unawareness

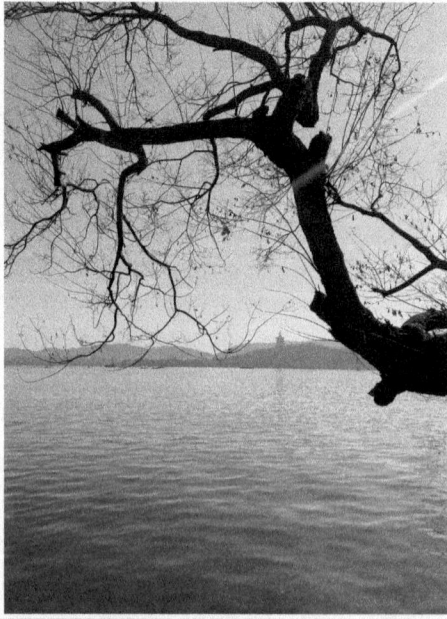

twelve.

there are so many couples strolling around right now
i cannot turn and not see
a couple
i cannot look at a man and there won't be
a girl attached
where are the singles?
where are the gays?
where are the friends?
what bullcrap this is
paired up like fucking noah's arc

i look inside a restaurant and see
a pair of people eating
it is a young man
baseball cap
a tattoo peeking out of his collar
his smooth oval face graced with
flushed high cheekbones and
olives for eyes
his mouth a set line
across from him is an elderly man in a tan bucket hat
sprigs of white hair trying to escape
his eyes and mouth turned down
their expressions are both equally grateful and fueled by years of hurt
the way that only koreans can look both loving and wounded
at the same time
and i know that they're spending their christmas with
exactly the right person

the amount of time i get to see them is perhaps
a second and a half
but they're the couple i remember
the couple who aren't trying to impress

or be anything but who they are
and
however begrudgingly
accept it

thirteen.

as the last seconds of 2024 tick away
i open the door
and step onto the rooftop
into the new year

there are no fireworks
i hear no excited yelling or whooping
there is no one surrounding me
no countdown
no ball drop
no television
i have a small plastic cup of beer in my hand
as i look over my dark neighborhood
on the flank of namsan

new years in korea is a
family holiday
and i have no family here
my friends are not yet family enough
and the language not yet familiar enough
plus the country is in mourning
and fireworks have been banned this year

i smile at the smattering of stars above me
as i realize that 2025 is simply
the same
it is all just forward motion
whatever i set in motion in 2024
will carry on in 2025
and what i will solidify in 2025
will be built upon in 2026
and so on and so forth

so
forward motion
is what i will raise my plastic cup to
forward motion on what i've learned
forward motion on what i dream
forward motion on what i hope for
what i love on
i started a lot of random things in 2024
let's see how far forward motion will propel them

2024년
the year 2024

a small catalogue of thoughts
on forward motion
while traveling

by sabina petra

www.ingramcontent.com/pod-product-compliance
Lightning Source LLC
LaVergne TN
LVHW051602080426
835510LV00020B/3096